EASY INSTRUMENTAL DUETS   TRUMPETS

HIT SONGS FOR TWO

Arrangements by Peter Deneff

ISBN 978-1-5400-1279-1

HAL•LEONARD®

7777 W. BLUEMOUND RD. P.O. BOX 13819 MILWAUKEE, WI 53213

Visit Hal Leonard Online at
www.halleonard.com

CONTENTS

ALL ABOUT THAT BASS

TRUMPETS

Words and Music by KEVIN KADISH
and MEGHAN TRAINOR

ALL OF ME

TRUMPETS

Words and Music by JOHN STEPHENS
and TOBY GAD

BRAVE

TRUMPETS

Words and Music by SARA BAREILLES
and JACK ANTONOFF

BUDAPEST

TRUMPETS

Words and Music by GEORGE BARNETT
and JOEL POTT

(small notes optional)

To Coda ⊕

CAN'T STOP THE FEELING
from TROLLS

TRUMPETS

Words and Music by JUSTIN TIMBERLAKE,
MAX MARTIN and SHELLBACK

GRENADE

TRUMPETS

Words and Music by BRUNO MARS,
ARI LEVINE, PHILIP LAWRENCE,
BRODY BROWN, CLAUDE KELLY
and ANDREW WYATT

HEY, SOUL SISTER

TRUMPETS

Words and Music by PAT MONAHAN,
ESPEN LIND and AMUND BJORKLUND

HOME

TRUMPETS

Words and Music by GREG HOLDEN
and DREW PEARSON

I WILL WAIT

TRUMPETS

Words and Music by
MUMFORD & SONS

Moderately

LET HER GO

TRUMPETS

Words and Music by
MICHAEL DAVID ROSENBERG

LET IT GO

TRUMPETS

Words and Music by JAMES BAY
and PAUL BARRY

100 YEARS

TRUMPETS

Words and Music by
JOHN ONDRASIK

POKER FACE

TRUMPETS

Words and Music by STEFANI GERMANOTTA
and RedOne

Moderately

ROYALS

TRUMPETS

Words and Music by ELLA YELICH-O'CONNOR
and JOEL LITTLE

(small note optional)

SAY SOMETHING

TRUMPETS

Words and Music by IAN AXEL,
CHAD VACCARINO and MIKE CAMPBELL

SHAKE IT OFF

TRUMPETS

Words and Music by TAYLOR SWIFT,
MAX MARTIN and SHELLBACK

SHAPE OF YOU

TRUMPETS

Words and Music by ED SHEERAN,
KEVIN BRIGGS, KANDI BURRUSS,
TAMEKA COTTLE, STEVE MAC
and JOHNNY McDAID

Moderately fast

SKYFALL
from the Motion Picture SKYFALL

TRUMPETS

Words and Music by ADELE ADKINS
and PAUL EPWORTH

SOME NIGHTS

TRUMPETS

Words and Music by JEFF BHASKER,
ANDREW DOST, JACK ANTONOFF
and NATE RUESS

STAY WITH ME

TRUMPETS

Words and Music by SAM SMITH,
JAMES NAPIER, WILLIAM EDWARD PHILLIPS,
TOM PETTY and JEFF LYNNE

STORY OF MY LIFE

TRUMPETS

Words and Music by JAMIE SCOTT,
JOHN HENRY RYAN, JULIAN BUNETTA,
HARRY STYLES, LIAM PAYNE, LOUIS TOMLINSON,
NIALL HORAN and ZAIN MALIK

VIVA LA VIDA

TRUMPETS

Words and Music by GUY BERRYMAN,
JON BUCKLAND, WILL CHAMPION
and CHRIS MARTIN